Copyright © 2020 Chris Moore

All rights reserved. This book contains material protected under International and Federal Copyright Laws and Treaties. Any unauthorised reprint or use of this material is prohibited. No part of this book may be reproduced or transmitted in any form or by any means, electronic or mechanical, including photocopying, recording, or by any information storage and retrieval system without express written permission from the author.

Author: Chris Moore (The Dog-Mother)
Email: admin@hsedr.org.au

ISBN: 978-0-6487853-0-9

First edition, 2020

Dedicated to The original Hope Springs Gang: **Teddy, Shelby, Bailey & Melodie**

Table of Contents

Preface viii

Mack and George - Loved by Bec and Jerry 1

Blossom - Loved by Sylvie and David 3

Sandy - Loved by Grace 5

Peppa - Loved by Michelle 7

Jimmy - Loved by Angela 11

Ffion - Loved by Pam and Chris 13

Marly/Jojo - Loved by Shelley and Andrew 16

Blacky – Adored by Eva 21

Chloe and Cino - Loved by Chris and Ray
(and everyone who meets her) 25

Lily - Chasing Butterflies over the Rainbow Bridge 30

Gracie (Mrs Jones) - Loved by Kim and Jeff 32

Buddy/Tex - Loved by Linda 36

Isabelle and Matilda - Loved by Chris and Marty 39

Rosie – Loved by All – especially The Dogmother
and Dogfather 42

Bella and Bonnie – Loved by Kirsty 45

Chewie – Loved by Laurence, Andrew, Pixie
and Pussy Cats 48

Shayla and Brody – Loved by Teresa 51

Fluffy – Loved by Wendy and Maurie 53

Rufus – Loved by June and Peter 58

Digby – Firm Friends with Steve 60

Jazzy and Rufus – Loved by Anne and Derek 63

Ellie – Loved by Sally 65

Daisy – Loved by Deb and Ian 66

Winnie - Loved by Kim and Jeff 71

Roxy and Millie – Loved by Jo and Katrina and Family 76
and finally by Rose 76

Cricket/Ruby – Loved by Julie and Eddie 79

Cooper – Adored by Angela 81

Tucker – Adventuring at Hope Springs 84

Peppi – Loved by Jane 87

Bella – Loved by Louise 89

Buddy Boy – Loved by Angela to the end 90

Gracie and Cadbury – Loved by their new family.............92
Choco – Loved by Beth in Canberra................................95
Olly – Loved by Peter and family 98
Bonny and Blue – (now Lola and Luka)
Loved by Lindsey 100
Tilly and Diesel – Loved by Nardy and Millie 102
Chance (now Henry) – Loved by Shelley, Gypsy
and Jojo..104
Daisy – Loved by Ben and Storm...................................106
Sally (Adored by Jeff) 108
Molly, Benny and Peanut – Loved by Dorothy,
Mark and Austin)...112
Casey (now frolicking over the Rainbow Bridge)...........114
Jasper (in care at #helenshaven) 117
Pele (in care at #mylormanor) 119
Teddy (Adopted and loved by Chris, Neil and Zoe).......120
Little Mickey
(Adopted by Helen and Ron at #helenshaven)..............121
Bonsai Ninja (Number 1 Super Guy))............................123
Shadow – Living the life with Lonnie 131

Preface

Hope Springs Eternal rescues and rehomes small breed dogs. Sometimes dogs that come into care are not suitable candidates for adoption due to frailty, or health issues or age and they will retire in care with us.

We are a small group who have been in operation for 4 years now. In this time, we have found the best new homes for 50 little dogs. Our philosophies are:

- 🐾 To change the world for one dog at a time
- 🐾 Rather than adopting out dogs, we adopt in families

Our greatest joy is to see little dogs living the kind of life they should - loved, treasured and valued as a vital family member and we love to receive photos and updates on them all. This book is to celebrate the families and the love these 50 dogs have found.

Chapter 1

Mack and George – Loved by Bec and Jerry

Mack and George were our first ever rescues. They came from a backyard breeder who made beautiful babies with them but were required by Council to reduce the number of dogs they had.

Mack and George spent almost 9 months at Hope Springs and were very dearly loved. However, we realized that we could not keep helping other little dogs if we kept them and felt that they deserved their own special family – where the love was all theirs – so they were profiled for adoption and subsequently adopted by Bec and Jerry – who have provided this update:

The gorgeous Mack and George became the Witkowski Boys in September 2016. Mack previously known as Lord Mack when he resided at Hope Springs is now affectionately known as Mackey Moo Moo. He has always loved his cuddles and now also loves to play.

Gorgeous George - such a boy - has always liked rough and tumble but now never misses a chance of a Mum cuddle.

Beautiful boys and a much loved part of our family

Thank you Chris and Ray for choosing us
(even if we are Port Supporters)!

Chapter 2

Blossom – Loved by Sylvie and David

Blossom came to us when her elderly owners went into Nursing Care. She was fostered by Jill.

Blossom had Progressive Retinal Atrophy (PRA) which causes gradual blindness and I wondered whether we would be able to find her a new home.

I still remember Sylvie and David's application where they said: "I think she needs us and we need her". Those were the words I wanted to hear.

Blossom had the best and happiest life with Sylvie and David and Chrissy her little fur -sister. The family were later joined by Ruby as well.

David always stayed in touch and sent us regular pictures and stories about Blossom.

She did go completely blind – but it did not affect her enjoyment of her life.

Blossom sadly passed away earlier this year.

Chapter 3

Sandy – Loved by Grace

Sandy's elderly owner went into Nursing Care. Hew Owner's daughter took her, but the resident female dog did not approve of an addition to the family and made her feelings known!

Sandy was a dear girl and when Grace came along to meet her – it was a meeting of souls, immediately.

Sandy and Grace were inseparable for months and we had Sandy back for holidays a few times. Sandy had a beautiful soul. Grace stayed in touch and would send me lovely photos of Sandy. Often they would arrive when I needed cheering up most – and they never failed to make me smile.

She had a friend called Ralph who used to come and stay on occasions.

Sandy and Grace shared a special kind of love. We were so happy that they had found one another.

Sandy went to sleep for the last time in November 2017 at the age of 14. Run free sweet girl!

Chapter 4

Peppa – Loved by Michelle

Peppa was also picked up as a stray by Council. Pepp was a bit of a challenge for us as she took a dislike to some of our resident dogs and we had to keep them separated. Peppa escaped most areas we tried to contain her to! She had one adoption trial that didn't work out and we wondered whether we would find her the right family.

We were taking her home from another home visit – that wasn't going to be suitable as they had another dog – and we had a call from Michelle, making enquiries about her. As we were close by, I suggested we call in so that the family could meet her. I'm pretty sure it was reciprocal love at first sight. Michelle contacted me about two days later and insisted on paying the adoption fee right then and there – so she could be sure that we wouldn't take Peppa away. Strangely, the first family that

adopted her contacted us a few days in and said they'd made a terrible mistake, they missed her and wanted her back. I had to explain that she was on another adoption trial and I had no reason to ask for her

back. Sometimes, life works out the way it's meant to. I enjoy the photos of Peppa out on the bench with the boys when they're out playing lacrosse. Michelle says: "Well, it's been 2 ½ years since we officially adopted Peppa and what a ride it's been!

As soon as I laid my eyes on her, I knew she had found her forever home with us.

Miss P is the centre of attention all the time and she loves the hoomans in her life.

She has a good life here and is very spoilt. She loves going up the river, on the boat, running around our property, she loves the car, and going for drives!

She has dinner with Nanna and Poppa once a week where she gets her bowl of milk from Nan as her special treat.

This little girl is my everything and everyone knows it!

Miss P will often be so happy to greet her hoomans she has been known to wet her pants. It's incredibly funny how happy she gets to see you, even though it's only been half an hour since you saw her last, she carries on as though it's been days!

We still keep in contact with Chris and Ray via phone, texts, Instagram and visits! After all, without these two miracle workers, we wouldn't have our beloved Miss P. #trustysidekick #peppasplace

Chapter 5

Jimmy – Loved by Angela

Jimmy was picked up as a stray by the Council. It is possible that he was someone's much loved companion – but no-one came to claim him and he wasn't microchipped so it was impossible to know where he came from or who he belonged to.

Jimmy was adopted by Angela – who told me that Jimmy made her smile again after losing one of her beloved dog family members.

Jimmy loves food, Grandad and going out for a jaunt at the park.

Not only did Angela adopt from us – she has become a foster carer for us – she is an integral part of our team, and has a great way with dogs.

Angela says: Jimmy Jatz Cracker came to us when our hearts were so sad as we had not long lost Bella and we all missed her so much. Jimmy came for a visit and decided the minute he walked in the door that he was home. He made himself very comfortable on the lounge with Shelby and Zuzie and they showed him how much they wanted him to stay - it was just meant to be.

Chapter 6

Ffion – Loved by Pam and Chris

Ffion was left behind in a rental property when the family moved out. She was seen by a passer-by sitting forlornly in the window.

We were full at the time and the Dog-father would only contemplate taking another if I could find a foster family for her.

Pam had made contact about Peppa and I asked whether she would be interested in fostering our new little girl. We didn't know her name – so Pam and Chris named her.

Pam says: "We owe our little treasure, Fi, not only to Chris and Ray but to Michelle and Peppa. We were interested in Peppa but she was out on trial so Chris asked us to foster Fi and ... we failed, as 2 ½ years later she's still here. She has gone from a timid and extremely anxious dog to an amazing little dog with a huge personality. She makes us laugh every day!

Chapter 7

Marly/Jojo – Loved by Shelley and Andrew

Marly was bought as a wee pup by someone thinking they were getting a miniature fox terrier size dog. The owner lived in a very small unit – and the puppy kept growing and growing. The owner had some health issues that made toilet training and exercising a boisterous young pup difficult and approached us about finding her a new home. As she was quite timid and reserved, she was concerned that if she went to an animal shelter, she may not be adopted.

Marly (while she was with us) had two speeds – flat out playing and flat out sleeping. She loved the Dog-Father and thought Snowie was a squeaky toy. She picked her up in her mouth a couple of times (and naturally tiny Snow squawked – reinforcing that view.  We had to put Snowie and her kingdom somewhere else while we were at work so Marly didn't harass her.

I recall even Mel – who was pretty easy-going – jumping up on the deck rail to get away from the 'pesky puppy'.

Marly had a couple of go's at finding her new family. She was afraid of men and bit the husband of the first family we trialled her with when he tried to pick her up. Similarly, in the second home, she bonded closely with the other family dog and the Mum of the family – but not so much with the Father and son -so came back to us.

Coincidentally, I had an enquiry about her about two days before she was returned and I made contact to see whether they would like to meet her.

This family were very familiar with the Fox Terrier breed and were looking for a second to join their boy – George.

It was different right from the start. They gave Marly the time and space she needed to settle in and feel comfortable, safe and secure.

Jojo's Mum says: "Jojo (AKA Marly) was adopted in November 2016. Hard to believe it was that long ago. She has well and truly settled into the rural lifestyle in a family of fur, feathers and folks.

From a dog who was reluctant to be touched, and nervous around other critters, she is now a proper Princess who lords over her manor with great aplomb.

Thank you Chris and Ray Moore for all the work you do, and for matching her to our family.

Chapter 8

Blacky – Adored by Eva

Blacky lived in a small unit with his owner who was legally blind. There was no external space for him to go out to the toilet and his owner was unable to walk him – so he was forced to toilet inside – where she would subsequently step in it. This became too much for her to cope with and we were asked to assist.

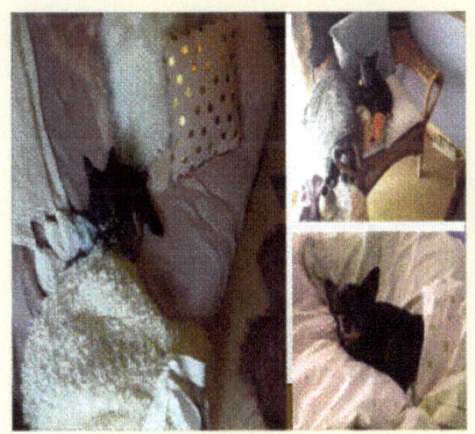

Coincidentally, I had been contacted just the evening before by Eva, who was looking for a Chihuahua companion as she had lost her previous dog to health issues and really missed the company.

Again a case of serendipity. We took Blacky straight to Eva and it was love at first sight.

Watching Blacky tear around Eva's big back garden with his toy tyre was wonderful.

He has a special spot by the window where he can watch the world go by and he takes the dogs each side to task – letting them know in no uncertain terms – that he is King of this particular piece of real estate!

Blacky says: Hi, I'm a little Chihuahua fellow. My name is Blacky and I have been adopted. I live in a lovely double story townhouse with my mum. I love posing with my mum. I think I am pretty photogenic.

I enjoy playing, especially with my toys and I have plenty of them. I especially love playing with my tyre.

I am very observant and everything around me catches my attention. I look at the world outside my window and bark at anything and anyone who goes by, even if it is only a little innocent ant.

I love sleeping in my mum's bed. It is so comfy! And I love sitting on the sofa upstairs with all the fluffy pillows!

I really enjoy watching the little telly!

I have an uncle ' Uncle Rom ' whom I adore and I love sitting on his lap and give him lots of kisses!

I am a happy, little chap and I love my world of wonder and beauty including my garden where I run around till I can't catch my breath chasing butterflies, lizards and an occasional mouse.

Oh, and I can't forget to mention my early morning long walks with my mum. Now, that's a must!

Yeah, life is good...!

Chapter 9

Chloe and Cino – Loved by Chris and Ray (and everyone who meets her)

We were asked whether we could help with rehoming Chloe (11) and Cino (14) as their owner was moving interstate. They were getting  older and although she had always taken them both with her previously, she felt that they were getting too old and would not settle well. She was also going to stay in an environment that was not necessarily welcoming of pets.

We noticed that Cino was rubbing his face a lot and crying in the night and thought he might have a bad tooth so we booked him in straight away for a dental. Sadly, he suffered a brain aneurysm and passed away in the clinic prior to the anaesthetic being administered. This came as a huge shock and I was totally devastated.

I thought when I received a message to call the clinic that they were just going to tell me it was going to cost more than I had anticipated. I was completely unprepared.

Chloe had been with Cino her whole life and was heartbroken without him. We decided that as she had become familiar with our other

dogs that it would be better for her to stay and continue to have their company. Also, Chloe had bonded quite strongly with us in the short time she'd been with us.

As an added bonus, her Mum was able to come and visit when she was back in the State.

Chloe is our little Princess, but sometimes she can be a bit of a mean girl to newcomers. Not that she'd fight with them - but she has perfected 'a look' and a snippy growl.

She is also known as Prinny and Butter-ball and Squirrel.

Although she's very sweet, Chloe does like some disgusting things like eating possum poo and dead flies!

Chapter 10

Lily – Chasing Butterflies over the Rainbow Bridge

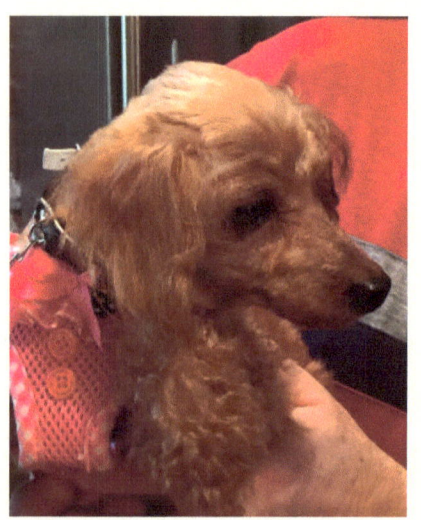

Both Lily and Gracie came to us via Marg who organised their freedom from a breeder interstate. They were both tiny poodles – Lily apricot and Gracie, black and silver.

For some reason we will not now know, Lily was intent on escape from the beginning. Perhaps she was in season and wanted to find a mate – or perhaps she was just confused about where she was and subsequently anxious.

Lily went to extraordinary lengths to chew the corner off a wooden board enough that she could get her paw in and create a gap, squeezed through the bars of a baby-gate, climbed a wire fence, and went under another fence to escape. She was sadly hit by a car, 5km's away from home.

We had thought she was safe – we were wrong. We've never forgiven ourselves for this tragedy – but we have learned from it. There have been numerous lessons learned along our rescue path – but this was one of the hardest.

Lily has a memorial marker and a beautiful apricot rose - "Remember Me"

Chapter 11

Gracie (Mrs Jones) – Loved by Kim and Jeff

Unbeknown to us, Gracie was pregnant when she arrived. Her and the Dogfather developed a very special relationship and a close bond. We cared for Gracie through her pregnancy and hoped that we would have some healthy babies that she could enjoy – as they would definitely be her last.

When the babies were born – The Dogfather was given naming rights – and he decided on Eddy (a little black boy) and Bettsie (a little grey girl).

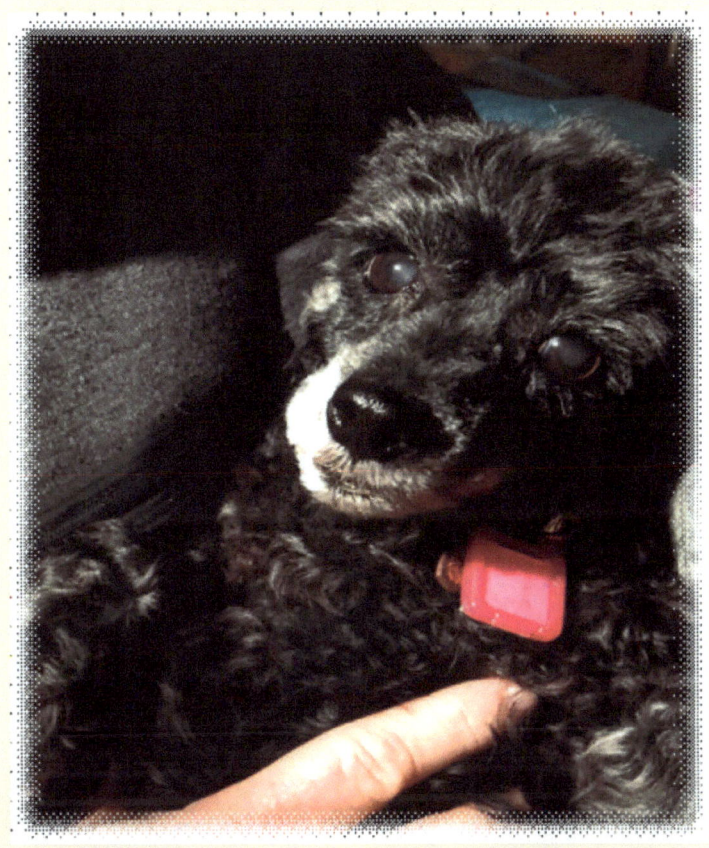

Sadly, they only lived a few days. Gracie was really too old to have babies and her health was compromised due to rotten teeth poisoning her blood-stream.

Gracie was so distraught when she lost her babies. Observing her grief was more heartbreaking than the grief we felt at losing the babies - who should have had their whole lives ahead of them.

Both have a special rose and marker in our Memorial Garden along with a black poodle Mama watching over them.

Gracie first had an unsuccessful adoption trial with a lady who had lost her husband and was lonely – but had never had a dog before. Gracie was subsequently adopted by Kim and Jeff and still comes to share special time with The Dogfather.

Chapter 12

Buddy/Tex – Loved by Linda

Buddy came to us via Angela. His owner went into Nursing Care and her family did not want Buddy. He was left to fend for himself against a much larger dog and had to fight for food – unsuccessfully – as Buddy was definitely NOT a fighter! Angela contacted us to see if we could help because the family were just going to open the gate and let him loose.

I met Linda before I met Buddy. Linda and I shared a mutual friend and when she was in SA visiting, she came to visit and made a donation to our rescue activities.

When Linda retired to SA and built her home, she was ready to add a dog to her life. She kept an eye on our

page and when she saw Buddy, she felt that he might be 'The One'.

Linda and Buddy (now Sexy Texy to some) are another perfect match. They have established their own shared living arrangements, understand one another's routines and habits and share a reciprocal love.

Linda says: It took us some time but Tex and I have worked out the rules of our relationship. It has involved some level of negotiation and in some cases, some compromise on both sides. He can be quite stubborn at times – but so can I! As an example, I have a rule that bones may only be chewed on the dog mat or outside. Tex wanted to chew his bone on the lounge. I said No – so Tex refused to chew it at all.

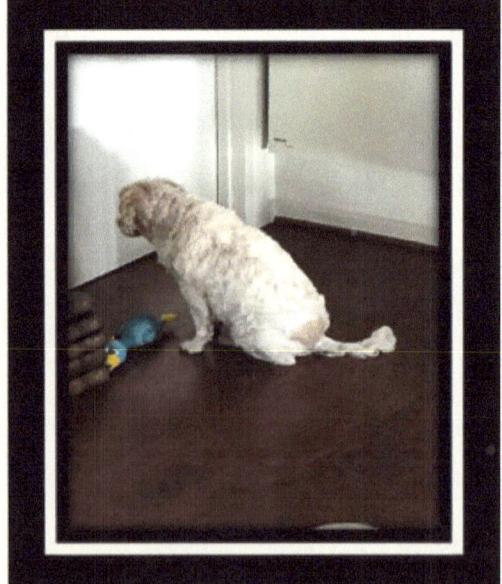

Sexy Texy is a great companion though and travels interstate with me to see my human kids who both adore him as well. He's a funny little guy. When we have guests staying, he'll wait outside the bedroom door with his chicken at the ready – to play as soon as they emerge. He adds a fabulous dimension to my life and I love his company.

Chapter 13

Isabelle and Matilda – Loved by Chris and Marty

Isabelle and Matilda came to us when their owner moved interstate and left them with her daughter. They didn't get on with the home-owner's dog where the daughter lived – so the arrangement couldn't be sustained.

When we went to pick them up, they barked the place down. I wondered how on earth we were going to cope with them – if that was what we were taking on.

They were quiet in the car. When we introduced them to the other dogs at home down the back, Matilda was so terrified, she jumped in the creek and The Dogfather had to follow – shoes and all to rescue her (another learning – we now don't do initial introductions down the back at all and all dogs first go down there on a lead and get shown around – before they are let loose).

We called these two The Bedbugs as they loved to get under the covers and go right down the bottom of the bed, where they'd stay all night. They were fine with us and loved to cuddle on the Dogfather's lap each evening. They would bark up a storm if anyone new arrived at home, though.

When they went out on adoption trial, they very nearly came back. Their constant barking was very wearing and pushed tolerance and patience to the limit. However, we agreed to extend the trial and with perseverance and love, these little girls created their space in their new family's lives and lived happily ever after. Mum and Dad have gates between their back garden and both their neighbours and it is a community – so Isabel (now Bella) and Matilda (now Tilly) have an extended family and three homes to receive love (and treats) from.

Chapter 14

Rosie – Loved by All – especially The Dogmother and Dogfather

We do not know why Rosie's owner chose to rehome as she appeared to love her dearly.

Rosie is the happiest and snuggliest dog we have ever met.

She did go out on adoption trial – but as she has a fondness for small things with feathers and fur – was returned for showing too much interest in the family guinea pig – falling off the top of the hutch and hurting her leg in the process.

There was some thought that she might require cruciate surgery, so we determined to keep her with us in case surgery and rehabilitation was required.

We both loved Rosie, she was one of the family and she was perfect for school presentations, promotions and for visits to retirement villages – so Rosie joined the Hope Springs Gang.

Everyone who meets her comments on how extraordinarily happy and cuddly she is – and many would love to take her home with them.

Rosie is variously known as Cracklin' Rosie, Wreck-it Rosie and Rosie Posie.

Rosie is very smart and works out how to get into things that the others don't even give a thought to. Her and Maisie encourage one another to consider naughty things such as harassing ducks or chasing rabbits.

Chapter 15

Bella and Bonnie – Loved by Kirsty

Bella and Bonnie were kept in the back-yard and used to produce puppies. They weren't valued enough to have a name each – both just referred to as Bella.

They epitomise the Cavalier breed – being sweet natured and easy going. They have been adopted by Mum, Kirsty who has seen to it that they are loved and treasured and now have the life they always should have had.

Mum Kirsty says: There are so many stories, fun times and photos that have been taken in our short time together so far! Like the time I came home to half the house covered in torn up toilet paper from the 24 pack that I'd bought!! Or seeing how excited they get when the leashes come out to go for a walk! But my favourite story is our first holiday caravanning together! We went away at Easter and had a fantastic time! Lots of laying around sleeping in the sun, going for walks and plenty of pats from almost everyone at the caravan park!! Unfortunately, on the Easter Sunday Bella got sick with a Bowel Obstruction & I had to drive back to Adelaide to take her to the Emergency Vet!! Not quite the end to the trip we were hoping for but while we were away, we had a great time & look forward to it being our annual trip together. Sadly, Bonnie passed away a little while ago, leaving both Kirsty and Bella quite sad.

Chapter 16

Chewie – Loved by Laurence, Andrew, Pixie and Pussy Cats

Chewie spent his entire life with one family but when they moved to a property in the country without fencing and with chooks – it became difficult for Chewie who was going progressively blind with Progressive Retinal Atrophy (PRA) and had a penchant for chicken dinner! Poor Chewie had to be tied up which wasn't much fun. Between work and kids, the family didn't have the time to spend with Chewie and felt that it would be better for him to go to a contained suburban backyard where he was safe and secure.

Initially, he came to Hope Springs but the creek was a problem for him. After falling into the creek several times, we organised for him to go and stay with Laurence and Andrew and he has lived here happily ever since. He gets on well with Pixie and the pussy cats love sharing his bed.

Chewie loves a good walk at Laratinga Wetlands, where he makes up for his lack of sight by sniffing voraciously. He also likes to spend all day outside wandering and sniffing in the garden. He lets the family know when he is ready to come back in by woofing at the back door.

Sadly, we lost Chewie a little while ago. He's now enjoying the gardens over the Rainbow Bridge.

Chapter 17

Shayla and Brody – Loved by Teresa

Shayla and Brody lived with a family where their novelty had worn off. They were relegated outside and the family did not even realise when Shayla was pregnant until they found a dead puppy outside in 40 degrees heat.

Shayla and Brody are a gorgeous pair of bonded fluffies and are adored by their Mum, Teresa and the extended family.

Their family says: Eighteen months on - Brody and Shayla are the most wonderful and precious two gifts in our family, and we just love them to bits.

Chapter 18

Fluffy – Loved by Wendy and Maurie

Fluffy's Mum, Wendy says: Mr Fluffy, now Fluffy came into our lives in June 2017, aged 8 ½. We fell in love with this beautiful boy, immediately. His previous owner had him since he was a baby and sadly had to put him into care due to health reasons. He had been dearly loved.

After a week, we knew that he would spend the rest of his life with us. Fluffy wakes around 6.30am, then he thinks it is his job to wake his Dad by just a little pawing, followed by a lick behind Dads ear – there is no way he sleeps in!

Dad feeds him, then out into the garden to see what has happened overnight. Once indoors, he comes back to bed to wake Mum with puppy kisses, then sleeps to work up the energy to play with his toys.

Chapter 19

Rufus – Loved by June and Peter

Rufus lived with Fluffy and needed to find a new family when his owner had to move interstate for work.

Rufus went to live with June and Peter and quickly trained them to provide toast and bickies at morning tea time.

Following some health issues, Rufus became a little too strong for the family to handle and has now moved to retirement living with a couple of other dogs, country farm visits and walks on the beach.

Chapter 20

Digby – Firm Friends with Steve

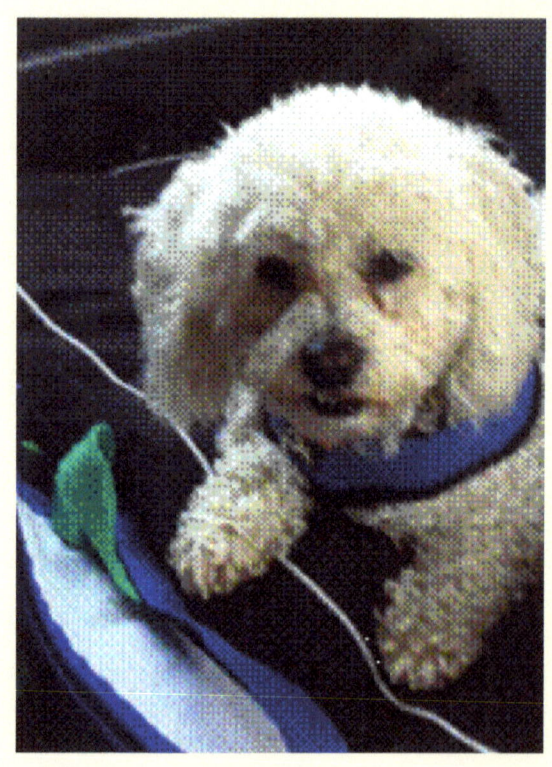

We were approached by a carer for another rescue to care for Digby for a few days while the foster carer went interstate for a holiday. As she was unable to deal with Digby, we ended up taking him on, and undertook to find him a new home.

Digby can be a very sweet dog and it is obvious he wants love and affection. He can also be very unpredictable and aggressive and has learned to use aggression when he does not wish to do something, or is unsure about something. Digby lived with an owner who had extremely high levels of anxiety and agoraphobia. She did not go out much and did not have many visitors – so Digby did not have much opportunity to become socialised. We don't know how he was treated but it reached a point where his owner could not control him and she gave him away on a for sale site.

We offered specialised behavioural training support to his new family to set them up for success. Digby had three adoption trials of varying lengths but all felt that they could not manage him long term - despite recognising that he wanted, and sought love and affection.

We wondered what on Earth we were going to do with him.

He could not stay with us indefinitely as he and one of our anxious dogs, amped each other's anxiety levels - making anxiety escalate for them both. We tried medication but this made him depressed and he isolated himself - which was really very sad.

It was about this time that we were contacted by Steve, who had a terminal illness and did not want to commit to adopting a dog as he didn't want to leave a problem for his family if he were to pass away. Steve was a timely god-send.

Digby and Steve have developed a bond and an understanding relationship

They've been together for nearly two years, and Steve tells me Digby is quite a character and actually lets his grand-kids rub his belly now.

Chapter 21

Jazzy and Rufus – Loved by Anne and Derek

Jazzy and Rufus (along with Daisy, Winnie and Ellie) came from a puppy farm. When the owner became very unwell, all dogs were rehomed via rescue groups.

Jazzy and Rufus had little experience interacting with people and had lived their whole lives in a kennel environment.

Jazzy showed her strong maternal instincts by gathering the toys bought for each dog when they came into care together and guarding them. She also enjoyed burying toys and garden gloves - and care had to be taken not to leave shoes and things on the floor or they'd end up outside - possible buried.

Jazzy absolutely adores Rufus who was more reticent than she. To see the two of them playing chasey (Jazzy was much faster than Rufus and would catch him by the tail or the back leg) and to run with absolute joy on their faces truly was a delight.

Mum Anne says: We adore our delightful dogs, Rufus and Jazzy, who came from a breeding place. We are so grateful and so happy especially to see the change in them from 10 months ago to present time.

We love both of them dearly however Rufus looks for Jazzy and me is Derek's girl. Out of cruelty comes loyalty and joy. It's certainly our joy ☺ ☺

Chapter 22

Ellie – Loved by Sally

Ellie went into foster care with Sally and her two little dogs Bailee and Mya. She slotted straight into their home (and Sally's heart) and it was really no surprise to hear that Sally wanted to adopt Ellie.

Ellie loves playing with her fur-sisters in the back garden, going on lots of walks and hanging out at the park with her other doggy friends.

Chapter 23

Daisy – Loved by Deb and Ian

Daisy was the most timid of the five dogs we took into care from a breeder. We decided she would benefit from some time with a foster carer in a home with less dogs, so she went into foster care with Katrina and family.

I'm pretty sure Deb and Ian fell in love with Daisy when they first saw her photo.

They came to meet her and decided they would love to give her a happy, loving home for the rest of her life.

Deb and Ian say: In February 2018, we were blessed with the opportunity to have Daisy in our lives (after losing our Sophie another rescue at 16) with help from Hope Springs Eternal Dog Rescue. Daisy was a breeding dog rescued when the owner of the property became quite ill. We collected her from Katrina (her foster carer) who has now become our friend. Here was this nervous little girl who was afraid of human touch and we were told about her not eating in front of people – and loads of other information passed our way that still couldn't prepare us for this little darling's needs.

 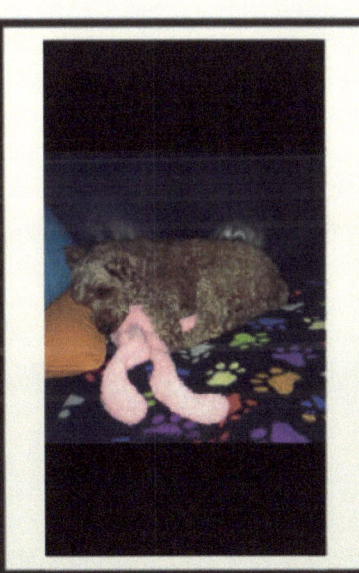 

Our first stop was Woolies for a BBQ chicken and this certainly did the trick to teach feeding from us! She found her "safe" spot in the corner of our lounge and that was it - she was home ✿♥. Next day a trip to the beach and we found her happy place - no other smells or sounds, no pressure just the reassurance of these people that "seem nice" and many new things to see and explore along the water's edge - a great day and very positive.

It was at this time that I think she chose Ian as her "human" she seemed to feel safe with him. With support and information from the vet and professional dog training confidence very slowly grew. We found the most amazing doggy daycare at K9 in Hayborough and with their wonderful knowledge and care they have helped Daisy blossom from the shy dog there to the now "leader" of the little dog session she takes part in every Monday!

There is a long way to go - yet almost every day there is something new that fills another part of our bursting hearts and also fills her "backpack" of confidence and new life!

She has even moved from the corner of the lounge! We accepted the challenge and the reward is great. The smile and THAT wagging tail make our efforts more than worthwhile. Daisy shares her love and trust but Ian is still her favourite person. This has been 10 months - where will she be in another 10? Watch this space!

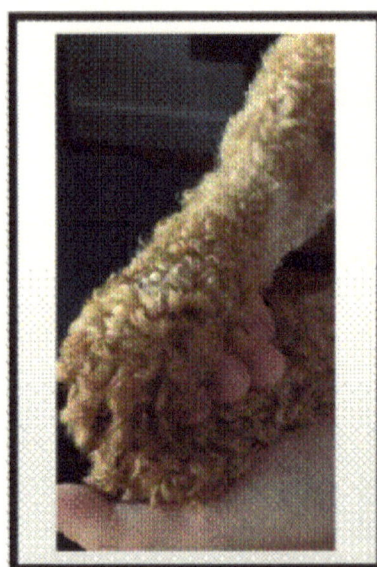  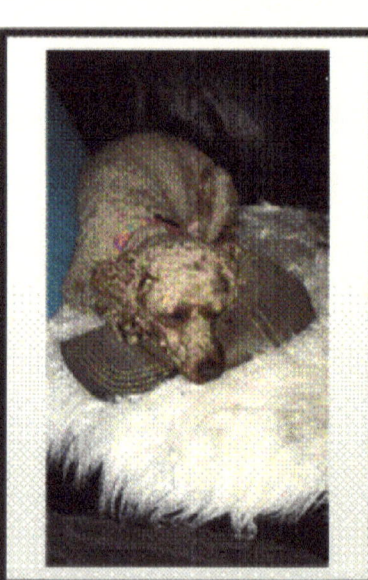

Chapter 24

Winnie – Loved by Kim and Jeff

Our story. Jeff and I got our first Moodle 7 years ago as a pup. We had no idea about rescue dogs or backyard breeders. We purchased this gorgeous pup after going to the RSPCA and the little pup we had our eye on went out the door as we were entering.

I had my heart set on a puppy and the other pups had all been adopted. So upon seeing an ad in the paper, off we went to 'have a look'. Oscar came home with us. Having failed IVF this little guy helped us to heal. He filled our lives so much. We travelled in a camper van several times throughout Australia and he was always at our side. After one of these trips we came back to Adelaide and it was time to expand the fur family. I had already met Jo who ran a rescue for older dogs. The Strathalbyn puppy farm had been raided by the amazing crew and rescuers with Oscars Law alongside RSPCA inspectors. Over 140 dogs were rescued from this abhorrent puppy farm. One of them a little blind poodle 🐩 girl called Dora who had recently given birth to yet another litter of pups at age 13. We applied to adopt Dora through Jo at Little Legs Dog Rescue and were so very fortunate to get approval. This little girl for all she had been through had the sweetest nature, she never once let her blindness get in the way of loving life. She would always be at our Oscars side. She battled two lots of mammary cancer and it really broke our hearts to have to let her have her wings as the cancer had spread too far at age 15.

The house was so quiet without Dora and our Oscar too missed her and would cry often. We then made the decision we needed to rescue another older dog. We contacted Jo who put us in contact with a wonderful lady Marg who knew about a gorgeous little rescue black poodle girl that was at Hope Springs. A little girl who has a very special place in the Dog Fathers heart. Gracie came

to us for a trial adoption. Of course she won us over immediately. She greets us every time we come home with her own little excited dance. In the morning we often get woken with nuzzles and licks. If we're home she will be sitting on one of our laps or snuggled in with Winnie and Oscar in the big doggie bed.

We then decided to try a stint at fostering. We were very lucky to get to foster a beautiful poodle boy we were given the privilege to name Rufus. He came to us very timid. We had him groomed and let him make himself at home. We did a foster swap as Rufus had to get his vet work done. Ray and Chris dropped off a little shih tzu girl called Winkie.

Another very timid girl. She loved to be a lap dog and snuggle and would have to share with Gracie who wasn't giving up any lap space. These two girls figured it out and have become quite close. We call them the troublesome two. Winkie went for a couple of meet and greets. She really wasn't interested. Part of my heart was breaking but I knew this was part of being a foster carer. I had told Winkie she was loved and there would always be a home with us. I recall Winkie then going back to Hope Springs for another meet and greet and my heart breaking. I told Chris and Ray the same as I told Winkie, she was welcome back anytime and if needs be, she always has a home with us. Well that's what happened - again she wasn't interested in a meet and greet and we are so blessed that Chris and Ray gave us a second opportunity to adopt another fur kid. She was a part of our family already. We renamed her Winnie. She's so loving and has a lot of cat like characteristics. She always meets us at the door and I swear she says hello. Our fur kids are our family and we wouldn't have it any other way. Oscar, Gracie and Winnie often go back and see the Dog Father and Dog Mother for their farm stay holidays and have a blast. Gracie and Ray get their precious time together (they have a very special bond), Oscar rolls in duck poo much to the displeasure of all around due to the smelly aftermath and whomever has to bath him and Winnie enjoys her choice of lap time between the Dog Mother and Dog Father.

Thank you Chris and Ray for fulfilling our family with the love of our very spoilt pooches.

Chapter 25

Roxy and Millie – Loved by Jo and Katrina and Family and finally by Rose

Roxy and Millie came into our care when their previous owner was moving to a retirement village that did not allow for pets. They were going to be put to sleep until the owner's grand-daughter suggested that surrendering them to rescue was an alternate option.

The girls went into foster care with Katrina and her family. Initially, they were in quite a bad way and required significant vet-work and lots of love.

They went out on adoption trial with a lovely lady who thought she was ready to add some dogs to her life – but ultimately wasn't ready, so they came back into care with Katrina.

We adopted them out in 2018 to Jo, a lovely lady, who loved them and gained a great deal of joy from having them in her life. We thought that was it for them -but then heard that Jo was terminally ill in hospital and the family couldn't keep Roxy and Millie - so the girls returned to Katrina yet again.

It took a little while but eventually after meeting quite a number of other potential families - Rose came to visit and it was evident that THIS was the family that Katrina had been waiting for!

Roxy and Millie are totally adored by Rose and Dave.

They are totally spoilt and have the best life imaginable. Milly particularly likes to sit in the window and wait for Dave to get home from work.

Chapter 26

Cricket/Ruby – Loved by Julie and Eddie

Cricket was only a baby at 5 months old when she came into care due to her owner being unwell and unable to provide her with the care and attention she needed. What I remember most about Cricket is that I could not get her to keep a warm jumper on (even when it was freezing) and the way she would go around and help herself to morsels of food from all the other dogs bowls – while they had their heads stuck in them. She also had a bark that was reminiscent of rapid machine gun fire. She always enjoyed another dog or person to cuddle up with when she wanted to have a sleep.

Julie, a work colleague expressed an interest in her and following a meet and greet with her and Eddie, her dog – Ruby as she was renamed was adopted.

Chapter 27

Cooper – Adored by Angela

Cooper was Angela's first foster dog. He was a tiny little sprite with a shaggy coat, a killer smile and a lot to say! Cooper too, is still very young but his confidence grew in leaps and bounds in Angela's care and he soon wheedled his way into her bed and her heart.

Angela told me I needed to write Cooper's adoption profile and let people know he was ready for a new family as she was becoming very attached to him.

I did write the profile but I never published it – because I knew that Cooper was already home!

Angela says:

Early this year I lost Zuzie and I decided that I would just have 2 dogs. Then - along came Cooper and like Jimmy before him, he made it quite clear he was never leaving - and so I went back to having 3 dogs.

Jimmy and Cooper have brought so much joy in to my house I can't imagine what it would be like without them, and of course, Shelby. I didn't rescue them they rescued me - and - I will do it all over again! There will always be a bed, a bowl, and lots of love and cuddles for any little dog that's needs somewhere to call home.

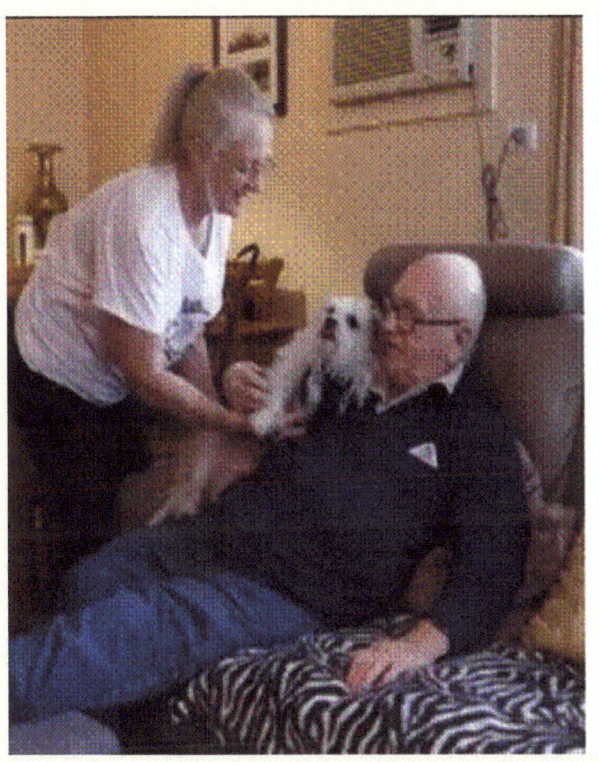 

Chapter 28

Tucker – Adventuring at Hope Springs

Tucker was surrendered to us by his family as he was constantly in fights with the family's other dog and family could no longer manage to keep them both.

Tucker very quickly attached himself to the Dog-Mother and made it very clear that he quite liked being part of the Hope Springs Gang and having lots of adventures at Hope Springs.

Additionally, his love of kids and his prowess with a soccer ball made him an excellent Ambassador at school presentations particularly - where he delights in the joy and laughter his soccer demonstrations bring.

Tucker is always playing ball or playing in the creek. He's a very busy little chap and likes to be on the go! He believes that visitors come to Hope Springs just to play ball with him - and will run off to get them a ball the minute they arrive!

Tucker loves sticking his head out of the car window and feeling the wind in his hair and on his face.

Chapter 29

Peppi – Loved by Jane

Peppi's Dad died and his family were unable to keep him because he just wasn't terribly fond of sharing his home with another dog – or with children – and both lived with his Dad's family.

Peppi had been a little spoilt by his Dad and consequently some of his manners were a little lacking.

Each night he liked to destroy a toy – not satisfied until he had removed its squeaker. He was a high energy hound who found it difficult to relax.

When the time came that he was ready to be adopted, a lady who had experience with foxy's and understood their personalities was found.

Her and Peppi have forged a strong bond and understanding and he is King of all he surveys at home.

Chapter 30

Bella – Loved by Louise

Bella came into our care when her owner (who loved her dearly) was forced to go into aged care due to her failing health. She had held on at home for as long as she possibly could because she was concerned about Bella and what would happen to her.

Bella's new owner, Louise says that she wasn't sure whether she wanted to get a Daschund or a Jack Russell (and Bella likely being a mix of the two) suited her perfectly.

The 2 ladies have established a fabulous relationship and Bella also enjoys the company of grandchildren and other family dogs who either come to stay or who she stays with when her Mum is away.

Chapter 31

Buddy Boy – Loved by Angela to the end

Buddy came into care with us when his owner could no longer care for him. Having lived the majority of his life as an only dog and not having experienced a lot of social interaction with other dogs or people, Buddy was somewhat uncomfortable about sharing his space with other dogs and people. He desperately wanted to be loved but was totally unused to receiving it.

He went into foster care with Angela. He was already taking medication for heart disease at this time. Although we tried Buddy with a potential adoptive family, it did not work out, and when he returned to Angela, Vets identified that his heart issues had progressed to a point where he did not have a long life ahead – and Angela and I decided together that he would remain with her.

Angela made a bucket list for Buddy and gave him many new experiences in the months he had. He went to the beach, he ate ice-cream and had lots of good times. Toward the end, Buddy was even thoroughly enjoying playing games of rough and tumble with Cooper and Olly, another little dog Angela fostered for us.

Angela knew when it was time and took Buddy to see Doctor Derek. Just before he went, Buddy looked into Angela's eyes and nuzzled in to her – as if to say thank you, I love you.

Chapter 32

Gracie and Cadbury – Loved by their new family

Gracie and Cadbury came to us following a move by their owner into temporary accommodation and uncertainty as to where she would end up.

The two were deeply bonded and Cadbury acted as Gracie's support – as she had recently become totally blind. When she was in unfamiliar terrain, he would go back and lead her on a safe path.

Apparently, howling is a cocker spaniel trait and Gracie was expert at it. She did not like to be left out of things and would howl up a storm if she thought that she was missing out or had been left in the garden whilst others were having fun. A cocker spaniel rescue refers to this as 'singing the song of my people'. Cadbury learnt this from her – and he too, would howl if he were left home alone.

Gracie amazed me with her resilience and her adaptability though, By the second day with us, she had not only learnt where the (small) dog door was – but was using it and able to navigate her way up and down the multiple sets of stairs at our house. She is a loving affectionate girl and her tail never stops wagging.

Gracie and Cadbury have been adopted by a lovely couple who have spared no expense in having their health checked and various issues attended to. They also have another poodle sister and the three are firm friends.

My favourite story is the one her new Dad tells – where he left a toasted cheese sandwich on his desk while he went to get something – and Gracie wolfed it down – there is certainly nothing wrong with her nose!

Chapter 33

Choco – Loved by Beth in Canberra

Choco was one of our 'six pack of chihuahuas' (Choco, Olly, Tilly, Diesel, Bonny and Blue). All came into care from a breeder who passed away.

We quickly discovered that some had very little interaction with people or living in a home environment – being more familiar with a small kennel environment.

Choco, Olly and Diesel didn't like one another much and we had to keep them in individual crates while they ate, and at night. For this reason, we decided to place some of them with foster carers so they could all get some individual care and attention.

 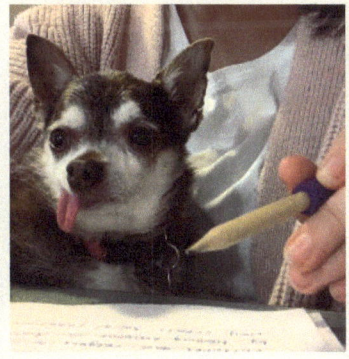 

Choco went into care with Susan. He was full of character and decided in the first couple of days to go off on an adventure round the neighbourhood – getting quite a long way away for such a little chap, and totally endearing himself to the family who found him, and cared for him, until I could let Sue know where he was and she could pick him up.

He also decided to "take over" the resident dog, Billie's rather large and sumptuous bed – leaving her with his much smaller piece of real estate to squish into.

We had numerous applications for Choco but neither Sue nor I could go past Beth. She emailed, submitted an application and rang to enquire about this charismatic little chappie and even though a flight interstate was not our preferred arrangement, it was decided that our International Man of Mystery would in fact go adventuring interstate.

New Mum Beth adores Choco and he's endeared himself to the whole family. Beth calls him: Guacamole el Guapo Guadalupe Gonzaga Gimienez. #ayychihuahua #micorazon #choccywoccywoowoo

Chapter 34

Olly – Loved by Peter and family

Little Olly is only a young fella at 2! He first went into foster care with Lesley but she felt he wasn't happy and so we placed him with Angela. He loved playing with Cooper and Buddy at Angela's and settled in right away.

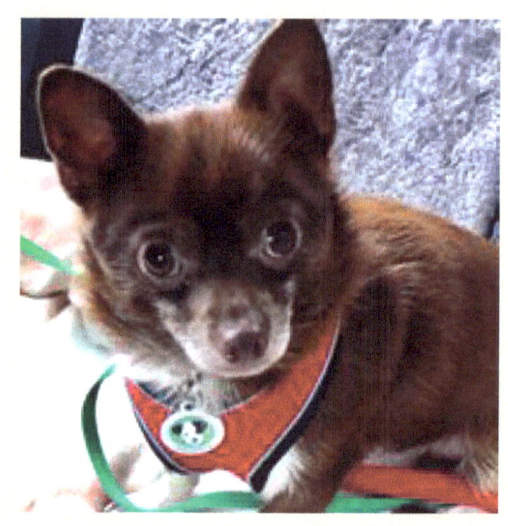

We found Olly a wonderful family that wanted to adopt him and make him part of the family and we thought it was perfect.

Sadly, Olly was not comfortable about the resident dog playing with his toys. It made him very anxious and defensive and so, Angela went and picked him up.

We needed Angela to take Bonny and Blue for us – so I organised for

Olly to go and stay with Sue. He bonded quite strongly with Sue almost immediately and she determined that he really needed to get settled in his own family where he could settle and establish a long lasting relationship and bond.

Olly has found that with Peter and family and has another Chihuahua buddy that he plays with constantly.

Chapter 35

Bonny and Blue – (now Lola and Luka) Loved by Lindsey

Lola and Luka were the most timid and least socialized of six chihuahuas who came into our care from a breeder. They are brother and sister and quite bonded to one another - with Lola being the more confident of the two.

They were absolute escape artists (lead astray mostly by Lola) and caused much anxiety and grief to Foster Carer,

Katrina. On one occasion, they got out and could not be found anywhere. They brought themselves home at 2am in the morning and loudly announced their return by barking – amazing given they were right out in the countryside!

Lindsey has taken on these two and although it has been quite slow going – she has been very committed to them.

Chapter 36

Tilly and Diesel – Loved by Nardy and Millie

Tilly and Diesel are like a little old married couple. They are never far apart and are totally devoted to one another.

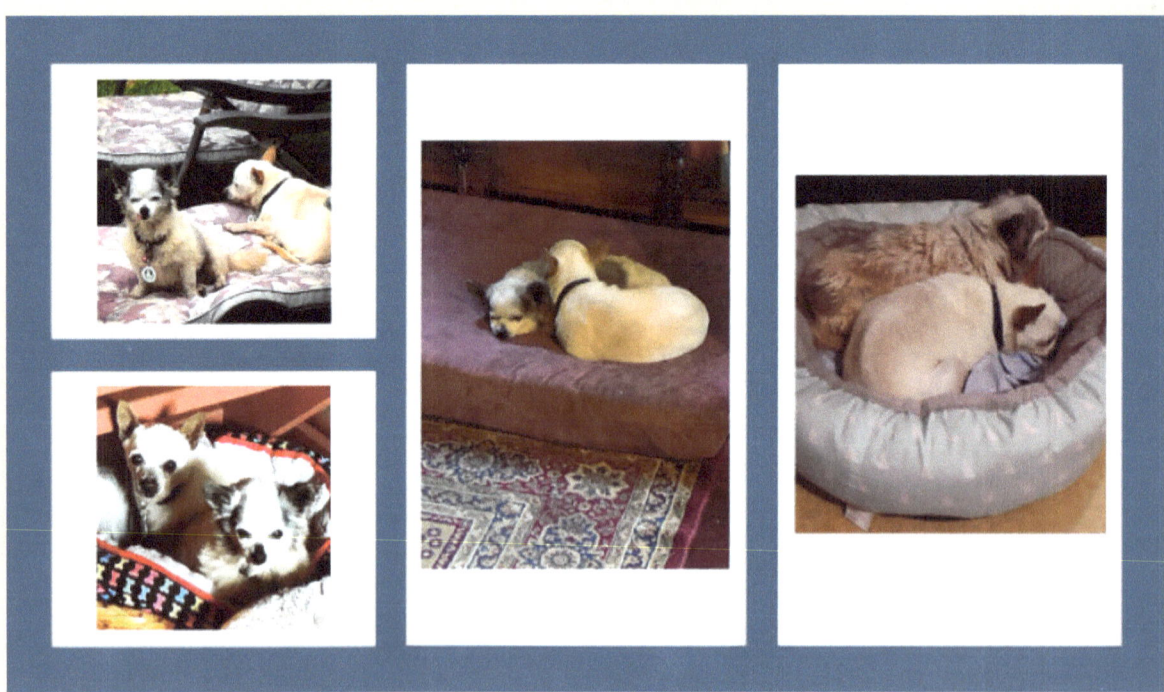

Tilly loves her tucker and the two of them seek a comfy lap and a cuddle each evening after dinner until bed-time with the occasional drink in between snoozing.

Diesel loves his sleep and he could snore for the Olympics.

Tilly is like Goldilocks and likes to try every bed in the house.

Tilly and Diesel have been adopted by Millie and Nardy and love going for regular jaunts to the dog park. They have their own Instagram and they own it! They have a few emerging health issues associated with their age but still enjoy their lives together with their family.

Chapter 37

Chance (now Henry) – Loved by Shelley, Gypsy and Jojo

Chance's dad went into care and the family were not in a position to keep him.

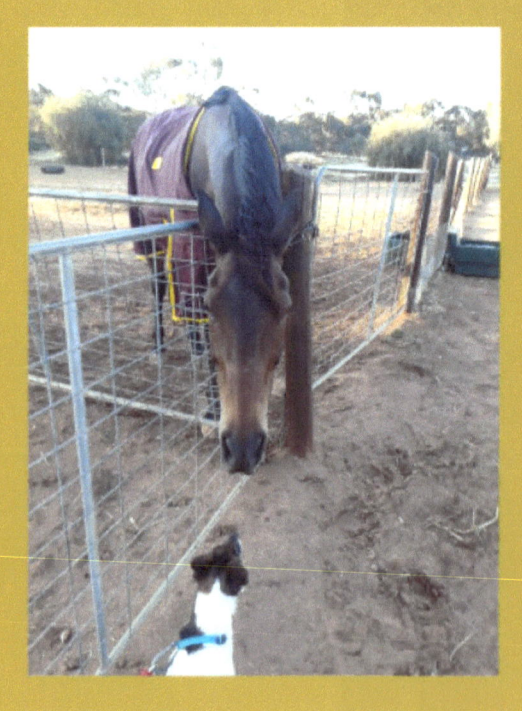

When I heard that he was a standard Fox Terrier, I wondered whether Shelley (who adopted Jojo) from us might be interested. My only concern was that Shelley had cats – and Chance apparently did not like cats!

Henry took to life on the farm very happily and gets on very well with his two sisters. He has learnt to respect the cats. He enjoys watching the chickens and getting out with the horses.

Chapter 38

Daisy – Loved by Ben and Storm

Daisy came into our care when her family fell on hard times and couldn't afford to keep her.

When Ben saw her – he fell in love immediately and filled out the adoption application straight away. We were a little concerned about Ben's other dog, Storm – who is huge – and thought Daisy might be frightened of him – but our worries were needless. Daisy rules the roost and has trained Storm to accept her sense of inflated entitlement!

Chapter 39

Sally (Adored by Jeff)

Sally came to us as a result of anxiety. Her family did everything they could but Sally's anxiety caused her to bark at the neighbour especially when he used any tools. This annoyed him immensely and put a big strain on neighbourly relations.

The family were beside themselves. Hope Springs doesn't normally rehome larger dogs or working breed dogs - but when I heard that Sally would have to go into a boarding kennel until other arrangements could be made to find her a foster carer - I asked Katrina if she could take her for us (starting that afternoon). Luckily our team are fabulous like that and Sally was duly dropped off.

She was incredibly sad the first few days and barely moved from under the trailer where she had parked herself. She also wasn't' eating and we were quite concerned. Both the father of the household, Wayne and Jamie, the young man of the house took Sally walking, and this was her happy place. Gradually, she settled and joined the rest of the family, keeping Dad Wayne company in the study while he worked.

When Jeff contacted me regarding Sally we had a good honest chat about her needs. Jeff sounded perfect. He came up to meet Sally with his daughter and Sally was comfortable with him right from the beginning. Sally commenced an adoption trial with Jeff and has not looked back. Her and Jeff adore one another and take long walks together each day. Sally also goes on road trips with Jeff to stay with his family on land in the high country.

When Jeff met Sally – the perfect love story commenced

Chapter 40

Molly, Benny and Peanut
(Loved by Dorothy, Mark and Austin)

Molly, Benny and Peanut all came from the same family. Their mum passed away and they were adopted to Dorothy and Mark by Hope Springs.

Dorothy and Mark made contact with the previous owner's children and meet up with them regularly so that they can still see the dogs. Sadly, Molly developed Lymphoma and has passed away since they've been adopted.

Chapter 41

Casey (now frolicking over the Rainbow Bridge)

Casey's Mum had to move interstate for work and left Casey in the car of friends. When Casey got out and was picked up by the Council, the family were advised that they needed to obtain emergency vet care for the health issues that Casey was obviously experiencing.

As neither the family or Casey's Mum could afford the vet care she needed – Hope Springs was asked to help.

Casey had a number of mammary tumours including an enormous one. We had hoped that this could be removed and that she could be adopted and live quite a few more years.

Sadly, our vets discovered that Casey's cancer had spread to her lungs and surgery was not an option for her. We were advised that she would only have a few weeks or months. We were devastated but resolved that we would make her remaining time comfortable and happy.

Casey loved rolling around on her back on the grass, had a great appetite, loved walking and sniffing at Laratinga Wetlands and enjoyed a day at the beach – chasing seagulls, paddling in the waves, digging in the sand, meeting lots of people, kids and other dogs and eating icecream.

When her time came – we were there to hold her as she passed and she is now remembered in our Memorial Garden with a special rose and marker.

Chapter 42

Jasper (in care at #helenshaven)

Jasper's Mum also went interstate for work and left Jasper with her Mum. Mum however, was not well and had to go into hospital, leaving Jasper home alone in the back garden. The neighbours noticed this and phoned the RSPCA who made contact with his Mum to let her know she needed to make alternate care arrangements for him - which is when she contacted us.

After spending a couple of days at Hope Springs, Jasper went into retirement care with Helen at #helenshaven.

Jasper's Mum has been back to visit him and Helen adores him. He is mostly deaf and blind but still loves a good play with his toy and dinner time!

Chapter 43

Pele (in care at #mylormanor)

Pele is an 18 year old Poodle who came to use due to family breakdown and sale of the family home.

Pele is now in retirement care with Katrina and family at #mylormanor. He's a doddery old soul who is largely deaf and blind - but very happy at dinner time and when he catches Katrina's silhouette and knows she's close by.

Chapter 44

Teddy (Adopted and loved by Chris, Neil and Zoe)

Teddy's Mum moved interstate and couldn't take him as he was unable to travel the distance. Teddy initially had a number of problems when he came into care and we thought initially that he would be retiring with us – but once his problems were resolved with vet treatment, a change of diet and some firm love – we discovered that Teddy was highly adoptable!

Teddy has been adopted by Chris and Neil and Zoe and is now enjoying his happily ever after!

Chapter 45

Little Mickey
(Adopted by Helen and Ron at #helenshaven)

Little Mickey was only 6 weeks old when he came into our care. He came from a Chihuahua breeder who recognized that he had some physical issues and was going to euthanise him. A kind-hearted lady took him home but then discovered that she couldn't manage him and we were asked if we could help.

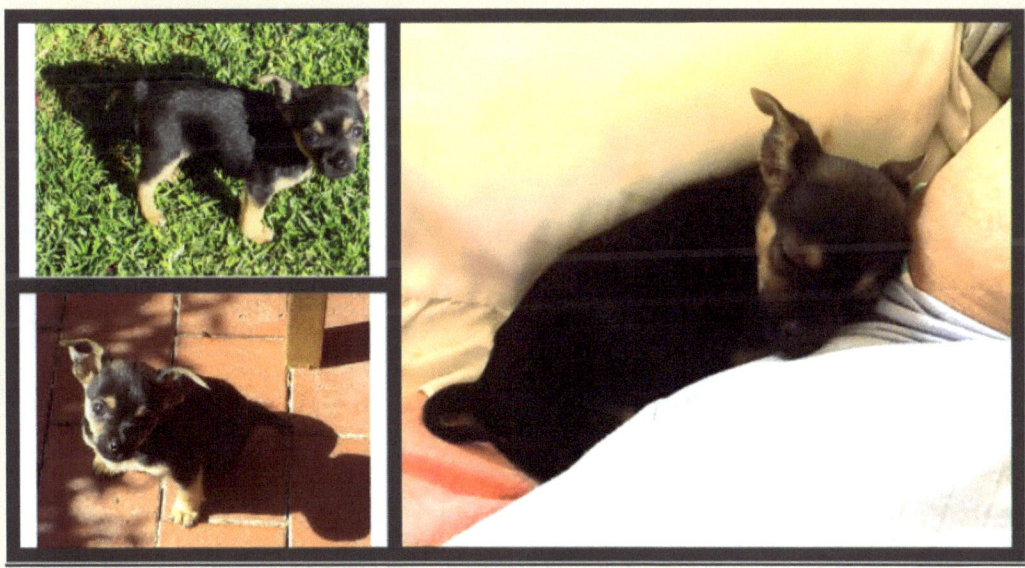

We weren't too sure what we would be taking on – but the Vet has indicated that Mickey doesn't need surgery and can live a very happy life

Helen has decided given Mickey's ongoing needs, she wants to make sure he's well taken care of – so her and husband, Ron have adopted Mickey.

Chapter 46

Bonsai Ninja (Number 1 Super Guy))

Though he is small - he is mighty! Bonsai Ninja is a tiny little guy but he has the heart of a lion, the attitude of a gangsta movie star and thinks he's a German Shepherd.

He lived a very spoilt and loved life with his Mum for his first eleven years but several things happened that rocked his world. First the dog he had spent his whole life with, passed away, then he stayed with a housesitter while his folks went overseas and developed a high level of anxiety and then the family had a baby - and when she got to the age where she was crawling - her unpredictability and noise made him very anxious - and according to his Ninja philosophy - with offence being the best form of defence - he snapped at her and caught her very near the eye. Although it broke her heart to do so, his Mum decided it would be better for Bonz to be rehomed as it was nigh on impossible to ensure the safety of both he and bub in an open plan home.

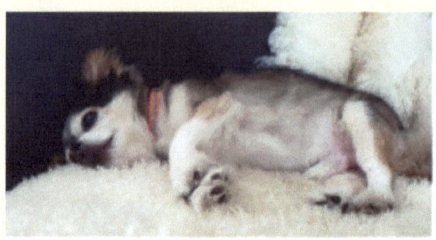

We were actually a bit frightened of Bonsai when we first met him – he showed us his Ninja moves and we were impressively afraid. We asked his Mum to put him in the car – and we kept a harness and lead on him the first couple of days so that we could move him without having to pick him up.

He went to #laurenceslodge🐕🐈 for a couple of days until we had his vet work done and then we took him to #suessanctuary. He didn't last long there though because he unsanctuarised #suessanctuary and wouldn't let her cats Derek and Claudia anywhere near the house. Each time he saw them – he'd chase them out again and they had to take up temporary residence at the neighbours.

So, we picked Bonsai up and he came to Hope Springs. I said to the foster carers – don't let him sleep on your bed and become top dog – but where did he sleep at Hope Springs – yes – on the bed – just while he was getting settled – he must still be getting settled – because he's still there!

There is something very endearing about Bonsai and he has both the Dogfather and I totally wrapped around his little paw. He has his own fan-club of ladies on Facebook who love seeing his posts.

He loves barking at the Emu – he goes down there with such purpose – he struts his stuff and = he 'owns' it! He's not afraid of horses, alpacas, or ducks – but he is a little afraid of the vacuum cleaner.

Straight after dinner – he's up on my lap and demanding his pats with a high 5. If for some strange reason that doesn't work – he'll try high 10! He loves licking the yoghurt container when I've had a yoghurt and . he's also very fond of scotch finger biscuits.

Bonsai has seizures – sometimes a lot – sometimes infrequently. For this reason, it was decided that he would remain at Hope Springs and join the Hope Springs Gang. Bonsai's Mum follows his antics on the Hope Springs page and on Instagram.

#bonsaininja   #thuglyf   #iwasmadeforthelyf   #minithug   #gangsta #gangnamstyle   #thebonz.

Chapter 47

Shadow – Living the life with Lonnie

Shadow was a stray cat taken in by Laurence. As she already has a number of cats, we are looking for the perfect retirement home for Shadow.

He's still waiting for his Happy Tail!

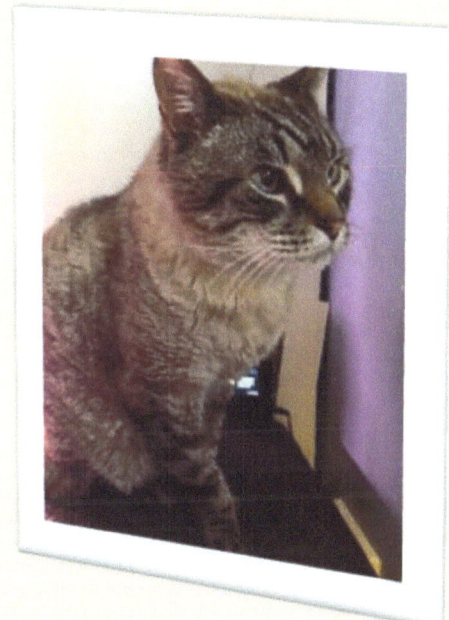

www.ingramcontent.com/pod-product-compliance
Lightning Source LLC
Chambersburg PA
CBHW041430010526
44107CB00045B/1559